POETIC PARODIES

By

Ken & David Kelsey

A tongue-in-cheek re-visiting
of well-known poems

K J Kelsey
kelsey@talk21.com

D Kelsey
david@kelsey.me.uk

Cover design
Jo Kelsey
Jo1208@hotmail.com

Contents

Contents continued

Foreword

By Ken Kelsey

Literary parodies go back to Ancient Greek times, with the plays of Aristophanes who lampooned the works of the Greek tragic playwrights, Aeschylus and Euripides. Shakespeare parodied and was himself parodied in return. The first book of parodies in verse was written by two brothers James and Horace Smith in 1812.

There are three grounds for parodying a poem. The first, where its pretentiousness cries out for the poem to be lampooned. The second, where the poem is a self parody, though here any re-working is more homage to the original than a parody of it. And the third, where a word, a line, a verse or a theme strikes a chord in a parodist's mind which encourages him or her to direct the poem along a different pathway. This book contains examples of all three, which has its origins in an internet game of table-tennis between, coincidentally, two brothers. David would ping me a parody and I would pong another back to him. Over time the numbers grew until we found that they were sufficient to fill a slim volume.

It was during this ping pong battle that David pointed out the similarity between two diverse poems, Longfellow's *The Wreck of the Hesperus* and Felicia Dorothea Hemans' *Casabianca*. In each of them the child of the vessel's captain, (in the first case a young girl called Annie and in the second case a young boy called Giocante) perished aboard the vessels because of the action or inaction of their respective fathers. In truth, the sources do not name the girl, but we felt that any girl with fairy-flax blue eyes, dawn of day cheeks, and hawthorn white bosom, surely would have been named Annie.

Scholars may deny that Giocante di Casabianca, of burning deck fame, was the childhood sweetheart of Annie, whose father was skipper of the schooner *Hesperus*, on the grounds that they lived 5000 miles and 40 years apart.. We take the view, however, that the spiritual values of Literature outweigh the materialism of Geography and History; and that Calliope, the muse of epic poetry, would have demanded that the young couple take their place in the pantheon of tragic lovers, alongside Abelard and Heloise, Pelleas and Melisande, Tristan and Isolde, Pyramus and Thisbe, and Romeo and Juliet.

So in the cause of romantic symmetry we have brought the couple together in a loving embrace by irreverently ending the original poems and imagining a wistful conversation between the two lovers in poems 12 and 13.

This book contains an equal number of contributions by David and me. I think his parodies are superior to mine and I think that he would say the same.

The last few words illustrate the quirkiness of the English language, for they can be read to convey directly opposite meanings, but if you like quirkiness, please read on.

*

1

To a Young Laundry-Maid

Gather ye soapsuds while ye may,
Your prune-like fingers plying,
But as you rub and scrub away
Remember time is flying.

The glorious lump of Hudson's soap
The chandler did deliver
Will lather down a slippery slope
And end as just a sliver.

The gentry upstairs in the house
Care nothing for your sorrow;
And though they do today carouse,
One day there'll be no morrow.

The washing's drying in the lea,
Your daily work is over,
The stable-lad is also free.
Make haste! Go meet your lover!

*

2

In Wordsworth's Footsteps

I wandered lonely, shunning crowds
That throng and press one in the town,
When all at once I saw the clouds.
They darkened and the rain came down,
Pelting and pouring cats and dogs,
Turning the meadows into bogs.

The rain continued for an hour;
I slipped and slithered in the mire.
A walker could not but be sour,
In such circumstances dire.
I groaned – and groaned – but little thought
What harm the rain to me had wrought.

For now as in my bed I lie,
With potions, poultices and pills,
I sorely rue the day that I
Went walking on those sodden hills,
Tempted by the poet who
I blame for giving me the flu.

*

3

Moley

Under the earth which covers me,
Black as the pit from pole to pole,
I thank whatever gods there be
That I'm a simple cuddly mole.

In the fell clutch of circumstance
I haven't scampered down my hole,
For Kenneth Grahame has changed the stance
Of this simple cuddly mole.

Beyond this place of wrath and tears,
Along with Ratty my friendly vole,
I close my eyes and give three cheers
That I'm a simple cuddly mole.

It matters not how strait the gate,
How charged with punishment the scroll,
For children always will relate
To this simple cuddly mole.

*

4

Beyond Comparison

Shall I compare thee to a brewer's dray?
Thou art less welcome and less moveable.
You I wish gone; it I do wish to stay.
All in all thou art less loveable.

I greatly do admire the noble horse,
That pulls the dray and thus doth prove his worth;
Whilst you with visage glum and manner coarse,
Have yet to justify your place on Earth.

Bass, Charrington, or Watneys all contrive
To render life more liveable and gay.
Without you I could cheerfully survive.
I wish to God that you would go away.

So long as I can drink and sup my beer,
So long would I not care you were not here.

*

5

A Modern Wooing

Come live with me and be my love,
And wash my shirts and cook my food,
While I shall my devotion prove
With embraces rough and crude.

And you can find a job, part-time.
My benefits will do for me
Until the happy day when I'm
A winner of the lottery.

And when I get back from the pub,
Where I have been most of the day,
We can order in some grub
From the local takeaway.

And sitting each upon a chair
(From DFS on HP bought),
For hours we shall sit and stare
And watch whatever's on Sky Sport.

So come on now, what do you say?
Come live with me and be my love,
And you can have me every day.
Surely that should be enough?

*

6

Home Thoughts from a Hospital Bed

Oh, to be in traction now the bones are set,
And as I lie in traction I can see in retrospect
That the traffic cones and the go-slow signs
Should have registered in my mind
That unless I slowed my speed somehow
I'd end in traction – now.

After the crash the police discerned
The skid-marks that my tyres had burned,
My bumper and headlights in the hedge,
Wings in the field, rear seats in the clover,
With wheels and hubcaps at the roadside edge –
Then I knew I'd be scuppered twice over.

Lest you think I could never recapture
The first fine careless rapture,
And though the police have issued a caution,
All will be well when I get my portion
Of the write-off value of my Lamborghini
And buy myself a Morris Mini.

*

7

The Hangover

A wet sheet and an aching head
And wind that follows fast,
Which fills the room, and so the bed,
With odours bound to last,
And eyes so blurred I think my sight
Is scarred beyond repair –
And all because I spent the night
In a pub near Leicester Square.

O for a soft and gentle hand
Upon my aching brow;
And give me a sip of something bland
To help me stand somehow;
And while the room is spinning round
And the floor's now low then high,
In my head regrets abound
And a sorry man am I.

There are cushions in the living room
And an armchair by the door,
But in this all-pervading gloom
I'd end up on the floor.
So back into the bed I'll fall,
To nurse my throbbing head,
And if I've any luck at all
I hope to wake up dead.

*

8

After Hamelin

Frau Piper was addressing her husband.

"Sigismund! More than a week have you been gone. Where been have you?"

"I've been in Hamelin, Liebchen."

"Hamelin? Where on earth is Hamelin?"

"Hamelin Town's in Brunswick, by famous Hanover city; the River Weser, deep and wide, washes its walls on the southern side; a pleasanter spot ....."

"Sigi! Enough! Very cross with you we are. Band practice on Wednesday you missed. Now that silly costume off you must take and your proper clothes must you put on."

"Liebchen, why are you jumbling up all your words?"

"Jumbling? What means you? This way how we Germans speak is."

"But Liebchen, this is to be read by English people in their own language."

"The English! Pah! Always their own way do they want. Now do you what I say."

Sigi stood there with a hangdog expression on his face.

Frau Piper was furious. "Do as I say!" she cried. "What waiting for you are?"

"We have a problem, Liebchen."

"A problem? What kind of problem?"

Sigi took her to the window and pointed. Outside in the street were boys and girls by the hundreds, all waiting patiently for Sigi's next move.

"Who on earth are they and what doing here are they?"

"They just followed me from Hamelin, that's all."

"Why here did you them bring?"

"I didn't mean to. I was supposed to take them to Koppelberg Hill which was meant to open up to let us through –   but it didn't, so I had to carry on home."

She looked at her husband accusingly. "Have you that weed again been smoking, Sigi? Of course open up the mountain didn't. What crazy ideas you have. Now do you as I say. Into your proper clothes get changed. To the urchins will I see."
She went to the door and confronted the children.
 "Off with you now be," she cried, "or the law on you will I have."
"But where are we supposed to go to, Misssus?"
"I don't know. Back to Hamelin, imagine I. Your parents wondering where you've got to must be. Already must they the Deutschenationalkinderschutzagentur be calling!"
"What is that, Missus? It sounds German."
"Of course German it is, dummkopf. In Germany are we not?"
"Missus, why are you jumbling up all your words?"
"That point already covered have I. Now go!"
She closed the front door, and reluctantly the children turned and began their long walk back home.
She went to where Sigi was waiting, now dressed in his proper clothes.
"Pen and paper to me bring," she commanded. "To Elizabeth need I to write about the trouble her husband with his poems to us is causing."

She paused. "And Sigi, back to the fancy dress shop that silly costume take. Next door to the Rathaus it is."

*

9

By Jingo

And did those feet from ancient time
Know that as centimetres they would end?
And that the English £.s.d.
Would to the metric pound descend?

And did our Government supine
Cosy up to foreign States?
And was tradition the price we paid
To please our European mates?

Bring back the peck, beloved bushel!
Bring me a hundredweight of coal!
Bring me my quart! O ancient fossil!
Bring me my rod, my perch, my pole!

I will not ease my gentle spite,
Nor shall a Euro cross my hand,
Till we have brought tradition back
To England's green and pleasant land.

*

10

Young Betty Williams

"You're too young, Betty Williams," the old man cried,
"To consider joining the Army.
You're still in your teens
And for me that just means
You are not only mad, you're quite barmy!"

"I know that I'm young," the maiden replied,
"But I've firmly made up my mind.
I'll find it exciting,
The training, the fighting.
I'll be leaving this dull world behind."

"But soldiers are rough," the old man went on.
"Their manners uncouth and quite shoddy.
You are too immature
And on one thing I'm sure,
They'll all be after your body."

"You're so wrong," responded the eager young girl,
"If you think college was innocent and merry.
One particular lecher
I sent off on a stretcher,
And I'm still in control of my cherry."

"They'll send you abroad," the old man declared.
"Mosquitoes, snakes and malaria.
Your skin will get leathery,
Your hair will turn feathery,
And your legs could even get hairier."

"Now, look, Dad," his daughter finally exclaimed,
"I know that you're going to miss me.
Jane will see to your food,
Ben will lighten your mood,
So now dry your eyes and just kiss me."

*

11

Benny

Benny fleeced me when we met,
Selling me some shares in satin;
Said the stock was bound to rise,
Even swore to that in Latin.
Now I'm bankrupt, hopping mad,
No ring left to throw my hat in.
Say it's my own fault, but add –
Benny fleeced me.

*

12

Hesperianca

The deck the boy was stood upon
Was where to his heart-felt shame,
He'd dropped the Christmas pudd upon.
The brandy well aflame.

The tar-besodden planking
Immediately caught fire,
Trapping the boy, now panicking,
To a certain funeral pyre.

Through seas both rough and treacherous
Now ploughed a masted schooner
It was the good ship Hesperus,
Battling to get there sooner.

The captain's daughter, lovely lass,
Was to the hapless boy be-spoken
And could not let the moment pass
Without love's final token.

As the schooner rammed the boat,
She jumped aboard the vessel,
And fearing not her death afloat,
Into his arms did nestle.

So died the luckless lovelorn pair,
Their tale now part of history,
While the rôle of the wayward Christmas fare
Now solves an age-old mystery.

*

13

Giocante and Annie

Annie	Giocante
My darling boy, one could not ask	I envy you, my Annie dear,
A happier fate than yours,	In those cool northern seas,
In gentle warming air to bask	Far from the torrid atmosphere
By Egypt's balmy shores.	Of waters such as these.
To save me going overboard	We voyaged from our native land
(The waves are rising fast),	To join a naval fray.
My father, with a length of cord,	Here father's ordered me to stand
Has bound me to the mast.	So here I'm bound to stay.
Oh Gio dear, I miss you now,	Oh Annie, if you were here now,
Long for your warm embrace.	To quench my burning ardour
Hot kisses on my icy brow	With your cool hand upon my brow,
Would thaw my frozen face.	*Mil gracias - De nada.*
I wish you here though I surmise	I wish, and this none can refute,
You come from Latin lands.	That you were here my sweet,
Sometimes a girl will not despise	To pour cold water on my suit,
Hot breath and clammy hands.	And some upon my feet.

14

Macbeth Today

To borrow, and to borrow, and to borrow,
Seems in this day and age the only way
To the class lifestyle that I see as mine.
During our yesterdays we had not learned
The way to run up debt. Out, out, work ethic!
Work's but a whopping con trick, a poor payer:
You strive and sweat eight hours every day,
And ask yourself what for. Why should I toil
And slave like an idiot, made to fetch and carry,
All for next to nothing?

*

15

So What About the Naughty Bailiff?

With a struggle a haughty Caliph,
Eyeing me with cold disdain,
Told me of a naughty bailiff
Whom, as things are, he'd not retain.

This bailiff used his strong position
To help young housewives sorely pressed,
But only on the sole condition
That they would grant him his request.

For while the tired wives, vainly breaking
Marriage vows relief to gain,
Far back police were quietly making
Plans to end his vicious reign.

Whilst lying with a Neasden widow,
When daylight came he saw blue lights,
And soon police were at the window,
Reading him his legal rights.

The moral of this story dour
To girls on matrimony set –
Beware of men exerting power,
Or, better still, stay out of debt.

*

16

Pub Fever

I must go down to the pub again,
To the friendly Rose and Crown,
And all I ask is a pint of ale
And change from half-a-crown;
And some peanuts, and some pickles,
Some salted potato crisps,
And a friendly glance from the buxom wench
With a smile upon her lips.

I must go down to the pub again
To answer the call of passion.
'Tis a wild call and a clear call
That always is in fashion;
And all I ask is a room upstairs
With its crisp white sheets awaiting,
And learn some French from the buxom wench
With bosoms now pulsating.

I must go back to my wife again,
To my steady married life,
To the dull way and my wife's way,
Where her wail's like a whetted knife;
And all I ask is an evening off
To the friendly Rose and Crown,
Where the buxom wench and this lusty tar
Find time for a quiet lie down.

*

17

In Digs

Kids' bicycles stand in the hall,
The staircase light is on the blink,
The paper's peeling off the wall,
And gruesome stains have marked the sink.
The woman who rents me the place
Does daily show her ugly face:
"Pay up, Pay up!" If I do not,
The greedy crone will steal my pot.

I'm kept awake by traffic noise,
And some kid coughing all the night
(Likely the one whose blinking toys
Make dangerous the unlit flight).
Here comes that awful witch again,
Who daily sings the same refrain:
"Pay up, Pay up!" If I do not,
The greedy crone will steal my pot.

*

How Poems are Born – an interlude in one act

[Spring, 1802. William and his sister Dorothy are in their sitting room in Dove Cottage, Grasmere.]

Dorothy: I have just been re-reading my diary entry for the day we walked by Ullswater, William. Do you remember that walk?

William: Remember it? I'll say I do. You'd darned my socks very badly, and they rubbed up blisters on my heels!

Dorothy: I'm sorry. But actually I was thinking, you know, that you might make a poem out of that walk.

William: A poem? Hmm, yes, how about:

> I went walking with my sister;
> Her clumsy darns gave me a blister.

Dorothy: *[a trifle haughtily]* I was thinking of something more idyllic, something about flowers perhaps.

William: Flowers? What flowers? I don't remember any flowers.

Dorothy: Oh William! There were buttercups, and . . .

William: Buttercups? Buttercups aren't flowers, they're weeds. You hate buttercups! You dig them up out of the lawn and put them on the compost heap, you know you do. I've seen you do it!

Dorothy: Well, all right, perhaps not buttercups then, but there were primroses, and cowslips, and ….

William: Really, Dot! What rhymes with 'primroses,' eh? Grim noses? What sort of poem would that be?

Dorothy: Well …

William: Or cowslips? Sow hips? Leave the poetry to me, Dot; it's not your forte.

Dorothy: All right. If you're not interested, I'll suggest it to Bobby.

William: Southey? Don't you dare! I don't want him horning in on my territory.

Dorothy: *[desperately]*: What about daffodils then? There are lots of rhymes for daffodils.

William: Daffodils? I don't remember any daffodils.

Dorothy: Yes you do; that old lady in the village was selling them.

William: So she was. Hmm, right, let's see:

> Daffodils, I bought a bunch
> Outside the place where we had lunch.

Dorothy: Oh William, can't you think of something a bit more romantic than that?

William: Actually, Dot, I've rather gone off that namby-pamby romantic stuff. I'm thinking of starting a new school of realist poetry. More manly, blunt, uncompromising, telling it how it is. Gutter verse.

Dorothy: That's all very well, William, but would it sell?

William: Sell? What care I if it sell or not? A true artist is above sordid commerce. Anyway, enough of this. I'm hungry. What's for tea? I fancy a nice piece of smoked haddock with two poached eggs.

Dorothy: There is no haddock, William, and no eggs either.

William: What! Why not? Have you forgotten to go shopping?

Dorothy: William, you haven't sold a poem in months. The tradesmen haven't been paid, and they refuse to give us any more credit. All there is is bread and jam.

William: *[aghast]:* Bread and jam?

Dorothy: Yes, and you'd better make the most of that, because it's the last of the jam.

William: *[swallows hard]*: Here, pass me your diary. I'll knock something up tonight and post it off to Longman in the morning.

CURTAIN

19

TV Critic

When I have fears that I may cease to see
TV programmes worth the while to view,
I wonder why it's a necessity
To air, all day, so trivial a brew.

When I behold, upon the TV screen,
The famous face of some non-entity,
Am I being asked to choose between
The image and the true identity?

And when I feel, presenters of the news,
That your bias and reality often clash,
I wonder if you're voicing deep-held views,
Or are you in it merely for the cash?

In this wide world am I alone in thinking
That most TV to nothingness is sinking?

*

20

Mayfair Lady

I have often walked down this street before,
But I wasn't looking out for men to meet before.
I'm so glad I've learned how much can be earned
Just by being on the street where you live.

I patrol my beat in the heart of town,
But you can find a tart in any other part of town -
In a corner pub, or a Bailey club,
Or out here on the street where you live.

From the gross income that I'm reaping
I pay most for food and for rent,
I give some to the man that I'm keeping,
And the vice squad takes its usual ten percent.

Every year I get an income tax rebate.
The inspector himself calls to help me get it straight.
He leaves satisfied that I've naught to hide,
Not out here on the street where you live.

Sometimes timid souls get a heart attack
When they spot me promenading in my see-through mac.
They don't realise it pays to advertise,
Working here on the street where you live.

But oh! the pious old fogies
Who want to keep my virtue intact,
And oh! the ambitious young bogies
Who want to do me for the Street Offences Act.

Being sent to court doesn't bother me,
For the magistrates are clients that I often see,
Who, when I am fined, let me pay in kind
And go back on the street where you live.

*

21

In the Old People's Home

When I was five and sixty
The Matron said to me,
"You know, you're far too frisky;
It's plain for all to see.
You gave Pearl a kiss, and Ruby,
And gave your Nancy three."
But I was five and sixty;
Why should that bother me?

When I was five and seventy
The Matron said again,
"You're at it still a-plenty,
It's bound to cause you pain.
Your energy will soon be gone,
Unable then to woo."
And now I'm five and eighty,
'Tis true! 'Tis true! 'Tis true!

*

22

Stock Excuses

You've heard tell as 'ow the Ramsbottoms
Best part of a day vainly spent
Looking for a "recumbent posture,"
Not having a clue what it meant.
They first tried their neighbour with no luck,
And then they tried many a shop;
No-one could supply what they wanted,
Not even the trusty co-op.
Now I am happy to tell you
Further details have since come to light
Of where they went after the co-op,
Hoping they might get it right.
Ramsbottoms next tried ironmongers,
Because it was only next door,
But manager said they sold so very few
They didn't stock postures no more.
He suggested they go to the junk shop
And try to get one second hand,
But the junk shop man said they were sold out,
Being in such high demand.
No matter what shop they went into,
Nowhere could they find one to buy;
But each one had a different reason
Why the item was not in supply.
Some said they were for export only.
A wide boy said he could assist
To get them one on the black market,
But there was a long waiting list.
The lady at artists' supplies shop,
Thinking perhaps they might mean
"Refulgent pastel," recommended
A large stick of virulent green.

They next thought they'd try Larkin's sweet shop,
Where Albert would buy sherbet dips.
When they asked for a recumbent posture,
Ma Larkin stood pursing her lips.
"Recumbent postures?" she queried,
"We don't have them quite precisely,
But we do have some redcurrant pastilles.
I should think they would do very nicely."
They went over the road to the printers,
Who sold paper and pencils and ink.
When he heard what they wanted, the foreman
Replied with a prodigious wink,
"Recumbent postures we've not got,
But following last month's election
We do have some redundant posters.
You're welcome to make a selection."

"Let's try the Red Lion," said Father,
But, not trusting his real intention,
Ma marched him to Methodist chapel
In hopes of divine intervention.
They prayed for a recumbent posture,
But they must have been misunderstood.
What they got was the incumbent pastor,
And he weren't a ha'porth of good.
They made some enquiries at Woolworths,
But girl there said, "You want a job!
You'll not get a recumbent posture
For a tanner or even a bob."
They then went next door to the meat shop.
Said butcher, "I'll tell you no lies,
Last one just went through the mincer
To be put in tomorrow's pork pies."
They had no more luck at fishmonger's.
He told them, with many regrets,
The trawler men daily assured him
They hadn't found one in their nets.

The lady at florists informed them
That supply was a seasonal thing,
And the best advice she could give them
Was to come back again in the Spring.
Pa asked for a recumbent posture
At newsagent's, only to hear
That owing to low circulation
It had ceased publication last year.
"Yesterday," said mechanic at bike shop,
"I'd have knocked you one up in a wink,
But today the unfortunate fact is
My torque wrench has gone on the blink."
The ladies at Sally Lunn's cake shop
Said to sell one was beyond their power.
They hadn't baked any that morning,
Having run out of self-raising flour.
Estate agent said, "I can find one.
Are you wanting it tiled or thatched?
And would you prefer end-of-terrace?
Or perhaps a nice semi-detached?"

At last they came to a chemist's –
Not Boots, it were Timothy White's.
Pa asked for a recumbent posture,
And the pharmacist set him to rights.

Mrs Ramsbottom left in high dudgeon;
You could see that her face was like thunder,
To think of the misapprehension
That they had been labouring under.

But Pa took a more sanguine outlook;
"Let's look on the bright side," he said.
"Now we know we can get one for nothing
Ev'ry night when we go up to bed!"

*

23

MARK ANTONY IN ROME.

Friends, Romans, Countrymen, lend me your ears;
I come to bury Caesar, not to praise him.
The evil that men do lives after them;
The good is oft interred with their bones;
So let it be with Caesar. The noble Brutus
Hath told you that Caesar was ambitious:
If it were so, it was a grievous fault,
And grievously hath Caesar answer'd it.
Here, under leave of Brutus and the rest –
For Brutus is an honourable man;
So are they all, all honourable men –
Come I to speak in Caesar's funeral.
He was my friend, faithful and just to me:
But Brutus says he was ambitious;
And Brutus is an honourable man.
He hath brought many captives home to Rome,
Whose ransoms did the general coffers fill:
Did this in Caesar seem ambitious?
When the poor have cried, Caesar hath wept;
Ambition should be made of sterner stuff:
Yet Brutus says he was ambitious;
And Brutus is an honourable man.
You all did see that on the Lupercal
I thrice presented him the kingly crown,
Which he did thrice refuse: was this ambition?
Yet Brutus says he was ambitious;
And, sure, he is an honourable man.
I speak not to disprove what Brutus spoke,
But here I am to speak what I do know.
You all did love him once, not without cause:
What cause withholds you then, to mourn for him?
O judgment! Thou art fled to brutish beasts,
And men have lost their reason. Bear with me;
My heart is in the coffin there with Caesar,
And I must pause till it come back to me.

Julius Caesar, Act III, Scene ii.

24

MARK ANTONY ON TOUR

Penge, Rodean, Cumberland, Tenby Broadstairs;
Pyecombe to Cirencester, not to Preston.
Yeovil Khatmandu Leeds Altrincham;
The Lowestoft Entebbe with Cologne;
So Wetherby with Pisa. Grenoble Luton
Hath Corfu that Pisa was Mauritius:
If it Thurso, it was St Peter Port,
And Peterlee hath Pisa Arlesford it.
Here, Sunderland of Luton Bucharest -
For Luton is a Barnstaple man;
So Hardwick Hall, all Barnstaple men -
Mumbai to Pekin Pisa's Liverpool.
He was Land's End, Bristol and Tuscany;
But Luton says he was Mauritius;
And Luton is a Barnstaple man.
He hath Portmeiron Cardiffs home to Rome,
Whose Grantham did the Jedburgh Huddersfield.
Widnes in Pisa seem Mauritius?
 When Jaipore Strathclyde, Pisa Morpeth.
Alfriston should Belgrade of Dusseldorf.
Yet Luton says he was Mauritius;
And Luton is a Barnstaple man.
Ewell Pitsea that on the Kiel Canal
I Guiseley Tenterden a Camden Town
Wheathampstead Syracuse: was this Alfriston?
Yet Luton says he was Mauritius;
Pershore, he is a Barnstaple man.
I Didcot to Peru what Basingstoke,
But here Vietnam to Didcot Idaho.
Ewell did Dublin once, Niagara Falls:
Vauxhall Cotswolds you then, to Warlingham?
O Plumstead! Stourhead to Cowdenbeath,
And men have Gloucester Beeston. Becontree;
Stuttgart is in Wisconsin there with Pisa,
And Ullapool till it Trincomalee.

Puglia Pisa, Ajax 3, Spurs 2

The Burglary We Done before We Took a Runner

Not a sound was heard, not a gasp or a sigh,
As we rendezvoused in the town centre;
Not a witness to see us with spying eye
At the pharmacy we planned to enter.

We burgled it darkly at dead of night,
The locks with our tools swiftly breaking;
The windows were shuttered, we turned on the light,
The drugs were there all for the taking.

No burglar alarm, no CCTV,
Not a bar nor a safe for protection,
But all the drugs lying there open and free -
We could take with no risk of detection.

We could remember when times had been bad -
When we'd had to scrape and to borrow;
So we steadfastly filled all the bags that we had,
And we happily thought of the morrow.

We thought, as we cleaned up where we'd been -
No fingerprints, no DNA -
Let the fuzz and forensics examine the scene,
We have literally got clean away!

Vainly they'll look for the clues that aren't there,
Not a scintilla of any traces.
They'll finally have to give up in despair
And file it among the cold cases.

When all of our joyful task was done,
And no drugs remained for the taking,
We heard a distant patrol car drone
And the siren noise it was making.

Swiftly and smartly we left at a sprint
From the scene of the crime - what a beauty!
We left not a hair, we left not a print,
But left laden down with the booty.

*

26

The Assyrian

The Assyrian crept up like a wolf on a deer,
And his troops were all hidden in camouflage gear.
From their matt weapons no light was reflected;
In this way they entered the town undetected.

The Angel of Death came too late to the fray;
Sennacherib's tactics had won him the day.
Hezekiah's army their arms had laid down,
And Assyrian flags flew over the town!

And the wives of Ashur loudly made their wassail,
And the candles were lit in the temple of Baal;
And the guile of the Gentile, his cunning invention,
Has melted the myth of divine intervention!

*

27

Brexit

Why so sad and mad, Remainer?
     Prithee, why so sad?
Why, when voting "out" was plainer,
You think the verdict mad?
     Prithee, just be glad.

Why so dull and mute, Abstainer?
     Prithee, why so mute?
You're now among the sad complainers
Joining the dispute.
     Prithee, follow suit.

Out! Out! For shame! That was the vote!
     Democrats! Accept it!
Though others move to rock the boat,
Hoping to reject it,
     Prithee, bring on Brexit.

*

28

Mobile Panic

When we two parted
At Heathrow, quite late,
I frantically darted
To gate number eight.

Once on the aircraft
I searched for my phone,
Dreading I'd left
The darn thing at home!

Pale grew my cheek and cold;
My body went numb.
Surely that fact foretold
Sorrow to come.

She'd open my iphone,
And quickly perceive
Those texts to Joan
I'd kept up my sleeve.

Oh God! And the pictures
Of Joan sexily posed!
There would be strictures
When she came to those.

During the morning
I fast comprehended
The very clear warning -
My marriage had ended.

My marriage vows broken
Beyond reclaim.
I could hear my name spoken
To undying shame.

A steward arrived
With the inflight snack.
Together we strived
To push my seat back.

He then said to me,
"Look, by your feet.
Your cell phone I see,
Sir, under the seat."

I could have embraced him,
American style;
Instead I just graced him
With my winning smile.

My marriage was saved,
Heaven be praised!
Though I'd misbehaved
My fear was erased.

When I do meet her
Upon my return,
How will I greet her?
We all love and learn.

*

29

Young Love Exhausted

Once did she hold me strictly at arm's length,
And was the passion of my boyhood life.
No lovelier person could ever be my wife,
So I pursued her with my utmost strength.

She was a maiden still, and hard to woo,
No way seduced, in Puritan estate;
But when she took unto herself a mate
She looked at me and calmly said, "You'll do."

Now we have six kids, her passion's stronger;
I'm knackered in so many different ways.
I harken back to earlier calmer days,
And wish her arm had been a metre longer.

*

30

AWAKE

AWAKE! for someone in the dead of night
Has flung a squib that's set your shed alight,
And Flo, your next door neighbour here, has called
The Fire Brigade to put the matter right.

But come with Old Khayyam and learn the best
Of all the mystic doings of the West;
But always bear in mind my Friends
That what I write I write in jest.

The little golf ball's hit, and being hit
Rolls on. Nor all your gesturing nor wit
Shall steer it closer to the hole it passes
Albeit by the tiniest bit.

Myself when young did eagerly smoke pot,
Tobacco, sage and quite a lot
Of other mind-enhancing drugs, but
What enlightenment I found I soon forgot.

Here with my iphone close upon my ear,
A can of Coke, a joint and you, my dear,
Astride me in our upstairs flat,
Then Paradise can wait another year.

*

31

Brucie

For years he'd taunted Wandsworth jail;
Then Justice said, 'A craftier male
On earth was never known;
This man I will example make;
He shall serve time, and I will take
All credit as my own.

'Myself will to this criminal be
Both law and order; and through me
This man, through punishment
Befit, and castigation coarse,
Shall feel an overwhelming force
To reform and repent.

'He's been as furtive as a fox
While stealing cars or picking locks
And various other things,
Like standing close to ATMs
Hoping to discern the PINs
Of unsuspecting beings.

'And vital feelings of regret
Will come too late for him to set
A credible defence.
For I have got his DNA
Supported, I am pleased to say,
By confessions from his fence.'

Thus Justice spake – the deed was done –
How soon our Bruce's race was run.
In jail for ten bleak years!
And now a calm and quiet scene
Exists where he had often been
And no-one sheds sad tears.

*

32

Barrow Boys

I struggled hemmed in by a crowd
That robs all shopping of its joys,
When all at once I heard the loud
Street cries of London barrow boys;
Beside the path, along the way,
Shouting their wares the livelong day.

Continuous as the stars that shine
In Lesser or in Greater Wain
They stretched in never-ending line
Along the margin of the lane:
Many a merry cockney fellow,
Along the road called Portobello.

People beside me bought; but I
Out-did them in a spending spree:
I found I could not help but buy,
Such was my gullibility:
I paid and paid but little thought
What worthless trash my cash had bought.

For oft, when valuing my stuff
And finding most is counterfeit,
I then decide I've had enough
Of buying from stalls in the street;
A habit which I find destroys
My faith in London barrow boys.

*

33

The Bowler's Hymn

Break, break, break,
On that balding patch, O Ball!
He's out of luck,
And out for a duck,
A valuable wicket to fall.

Swing, swing, swing,
In a lazy curving arc.
He's tried to sweep her,
And our trusty keeper
Has stumped him out of his mark.

Pitch, pitch, pitch,
Unexpectedly fast and low.
He's completely lost sight
Of the line of flight,
And we've seen another one go.

Spin, spin, spin,
With devious trickery.
He's tried to attack,
But he's played it straight back,
And that's him out c and b!

Hip, hip, hip,
And hooray for the joy that's mine!
I have bowled at my best
And the book will attest
That I've ended with four for nine!

*

34

To be sung to the tune of:

The Grand Old Duke of York

A man of repute in York
He had ten thousand yen
He bought some fixed yield Government Bonds
Which he re-sold at a gain
For the Bond price did go up
And the percentage yield go down
So to try to clean the market up
He did the market down.

*

35

The truth about the man from Porlock

Sam sat in his den contentedly puffing at his opium pipe, the clouds of smoke swirling around him.

"This is seriously good pot," he said to himself. "I could never have written this without the inspiration it gives me."

He gazed at the opening lines again:

> In Xanadu did Kubla Khan
> A stately pleasure dome decree,
> Where Alph, the sacred river, ran
> Through caverns measureless to man
> Down to a sunless sea.

He continued to read further until he reached the lines he had just written:

> And mid this tumult Kubla heard from far
> Ancestral voices prophesying war!

"This is my best poem so far," Sam mused. "Such imagery! Such vibrancy! When it's finished it will be hailed as a masterpiece."

There came a knock at the cottage door. "Who the hell can be calling at this time of day?" he grumbled as he rose to see who it was.

"Afternoon, Squire. Dan Fletcher at your service. I have a delivery for Samuel Coleridge Taylor."

"That is not I. I am Samuel Taylor Coleridge, a different person entirely."

"The lady down the lane said it is you and pointed out your cottage to me. The other name's not your pen name, is it?"

"Certainly not! I am not Samuel Coleridge Taylor. You must take the goods back."

"Have you seen Porlock Hill, Squire? It's seriously steep. It was easy enough getting here because it was downhill, but I can't see my horse and cart managing the uphill climb with three dozen brass curtain rods still on board."

"My good man, that is your problem, not mine. You must take them back."

"Squire, I'm paid to deliver goods, not take them back. They're here now so where shall I put them?"

He went to the back of the cart and began unknotting the rope that secured the rods.

"Now you look here!" Sam commanded, taking a threatening step forward.

Dan unbuttoned the cuffs of his shirt and rolled the sleeves up to his elbows. He turned to Sam and said, "You were saying, Squire?"

Sam acknowledged defeat. "OK, OK. I'll tell you the truth. I told a fib. I did order them but they're to be delivered elsewhere."

"Why the hell didn't you say so in the first place? Right, where are they to go? And if it involves Porlock Hill you can forget it."

"No, it's just a little further back down the lane. You know the lady who pointed out my cottage to you? Well, they're for her, a surprise. What I'd like you to do is lay them out quietly, one by one along the garden path to her cottage door. But quietly. She mustn't hear you otherwise it will spoil the surprise. OK?"

"OK, Squire. But they're not paid for. They're C.O.D."

Sam gasped. "How much?"

Dan consulted the paperwork. "Eighteen shillings and four pence three farthings."

Sam took an embroidered purse from the pocket of his silk dressing gown and counted the money out into Dan's outstretched hand. "One half sovereign, one crown, three pounds and four pence three farthings."

Dan looked at the coins in his hand but stood motionless.

"What?" asked Sam.

"What, no tip?"

Sam delved into his purse again and gave Dan a threepenny piece.

"That's very generous of you, Squire. You sure that other name's not your pen name? It could be, you know." He pocketed the money and turned his horse and cart around and retraced his steps along the lane.

Sam went back into the cottage drained. His wife, Sarah, entered the den.

"Who was that at the door, Dearest?" she asked.

"Oh, just some man asking directions."

"Pity. I was hoping it was the delivery of the brass curtain rods I had ordered. Dearest, are you alright? You've gone quite pale. Dearest, you're worrying me now with your shaking. Please sit down and calm yourself. Why don't you finish your poem?"

"The mood's gone," he complained, sulkily picking up his pipe. He stared into its bowl. "That's all gone too, and that's the last of my pot."

"Surely you can get some more, Dearest?"

"I'm not so sure now that Percy has gone to Greece."

"Well, try to finish your poem anyway."

Sam studied the paper. "Where was I?"

> And mid this tumult Kubla heard from far
> Ancestral voices prophesying war!

"I haven't the foggiest idea of what was to come after that. Without pot my imagination's not up to it!"

"Well, try anyway, Dearest."

He wrote a few more lines. "It's hopeless," he complained. "Listen to this:

> A damsel with a dulcimer
> In a vision I once saw.
> It was an Abyssinian maid
> And on her dulcimer she played.

What on earth's an Abyssinian maid doing in an ice-cold Mongolian pleasure dome, with or without a dulcimer? She wasn't in my vision an hour ago. It's hopeless, Sarah. The poem's ruined!"

"Finish it anyway, Dearest, but be quick. Dorothy and William said they may pop in later."

Sam continued to write without enthusiasm

Blah blah blah blah blah blah blah
Blah blah blah blah blah blah blah
And drunk the milk of Paradise.

"There! It's finished, but the publisher in London is bound to reject it. He will see it's not a single poem. I'll be a laughing stock!"

"Why don't you submit it under a nom de plume, then if the publisher thinks it's brilliant you can claim it as your own."

"Of course, Sarah. How right you are."

He seized his quill pen, dipped it into the inkwell and signed the poem:

"Samuel Coleridge Taylor"

*

Or alternatively:

36

Windows

In Xanadu did Kubla Khan
A stately pleasure-dome decree.
According to his final plan
The windows (there were 93)
All would double-glazèd be.

He'd been called on by a man
Who promised to install the best
Behind which he could ever rest
Assured of both security
And energy conservancy.

The hour grew late - the clock showed nine -
So Kubla signed upon the line.
At once his caller tugged his forelock
And swiftly went back home to Porlock.

*

37

Glory to Ashes Turned

O Captain! my Captain! The Ashes have been won.
The crowd have followed every ball, applauded every run.
The press is here, on hand to hear the people all exulting,
While Aussie eyes are wet with tears, their faces grim and sulking.
But O heart! heart! heart!
O the bleeding drops of luck,
Where here at Lords my Captain lies,
First ball. Another duck.

O Captain! my Captain! rise up and hear the cheers.
Rise up—for you the flag is flung—for you the best of years.
For you bouquets and ribbon'd wreaths—for you an honour earned,
For you they call, the swaying mass, their eager faces turned.
Here Captain! Dear Captain!
What's causing you despair?
Is it some dream that in the field
You've scored another pair?

My Captain does not answer, his lips are pale and still.
My Captain does not hear my words, he has no pulse nor will.
But though the Ashes now are safe, for four more years or more.
The memory that my Captain holds will haunt him evermore.
Exult O crowds, and ring O bells,
But I with mournful air
Walk the field my Captain scored
Another golden pair.

*

38

Football Fervour

Do not go gentle to the football match.
We fans should burn and rave at close of play;
Rage, rage against the win they snatched.

That linesman in his mind knew how to catch
Our man offside and ruled that goal away,
Do not go gentle to the football match.

The referee on a penalty did latch
And sent our centre forward on his way;
Rage, rage against the win they snatched.

Wild fans, the team's selection was not a patch
On what we could and should expect today;
Do not go gentle to the football match.

*

39

Wishes

I wish I loved my new computer,
I wish I loved my Windows 10,
I wish that I could fix the router
So I could e-mail now and then.
I wish that I had read the manual
'Bout joining laptop to the scanner.
I wish I'd not been quite so casual
About the engineer's brusque manner.
I wish I'd bought my anti-virus
Well before the latest scare.
I wish that Google would inspire us
To treat all updates with more care.
I wish, in fact, that I had listened
To my grandson based in Tring,
And sitting here with face all wizened
I wish I'd never bought the thing.

*

40

The Joys of Motoring

Slow bicycles ride side by side,
And round them I do peer in vain.
A lorry surely ten foot wide
Does grimly hog the centre lane.
There seems to be no way around,
And now I hear a siren sound:
Ne Nah, Ne Nah; an urgent noise.
What else but motoring brings such joys?

The satnav screen has run amuck,
And now here comes a steady rain.
The windscreen wiper's firmly stuck,
The oil light's come on again.
What else can possibly go wrong?
The cop car sings its strident song:
Ne Nah, Ne Nah; an urgent noise.
What else but motoring brings such joys?

*

41

On First Looking Into Bus Timetables

Much have I travelled on a London bus,
Round many Squares and Circuses have I been.
I've often caught the 83 to Golders Green
And rode the 61 to Bromley without fuss.

Oft of one route have I been told
Which goes from Hackney Wick to Marble Arch;
But when I tried to board the bus last March
I was told that all the tickets had been sold.

Then felt I a pedestrian at a loss
Torn between the 302 to Kensal Rise.
I didn't like that journey distance-wise
And preferred the 45 to Charing Cross.

The driver looked at me with mild surmise
And suggested I got off before South Ken;
So I went home aboard a number 10,
Silent at my peak of enterprise.

*

42

Death and Taxes

Must I pay taxes all of my life?
    Yes, to the very end.
How long must I work in endless strife?
    From morn to night, my friend.

Will you read with compassion the letters I write?
    It's never happened before.
Will my MP work to put things right?
    Not unless your account is off-shore.

Shall I find tax relief before I am dead?
    I cannot see how that can be.
Will I be free when I'm dead in my bed?
    No, you're forgetting about IHT.

*

43

Yesteryear in Parliament.

Speaker: Order! Order! Before proceedings begin I have a note for Members' diaries. The Minister for Lake Poets will be making a Statement upon Westminster Bridge on September 3rd, 1802. Now for today's business: Autumn Statement by the Minister for Romantic Poets. I call Minister John Keats. Minister!

Minister: Thank you, Mr Speaker. Today I am pleased to announce that this year we can all expect a Season of mists and mellow fruitfulness. *[cries of 'what about the workers']*

The Minister carried on with 'fruit the vines that round the thatch-eves run, until they think warm days will never cease for Summer has o'er-brimmed their clammy cells', and ending with,

'I commend this Poem to the House'.

Speaker: All those in favour, say Aye, those against say No. The Ayes have it, the Ayes have it.

In the public gallery a young Spanish art student named Pablo was sketching a human face. 'The eyes to the right,' he muttered, 'the nose to the left'.

*

44

Bought Love

My lover has a red, red nose
That's brought about by drink:
My lover to the bottle goes
More often than you'd think.

Though drunk he is, he'll always pay;
So deep in debt am I
That I'll stay with him, come what may,
Till all the gins run dry.

Till all the gins run dry, I say,
While he still pays my bills
I'll stay with him, night and day,
Till in the end drink kills.

Then, fare thee well, you drunken sot,
And thank you for your Will,
For it seems that I have copped the lot,
Just short of half a mill.

*

45

Old Age

Myself now old reluctantly frequent
Doctor and nurse, and take medicament -
Tablets, capsules, and pills - to ward off all the ills
There are, and some that they invent.
On them samples of blood do I bestow,
And multitudes of scans do undergo;
And this is all the answer that they give:
"When your time is up, then you will go."

*

46

Shop Fever

I must go down to the shops again,
To the local shops or the mall,
Or a corner shop or department store
 Or a humble market stall;
And all I ask is a place to park
Not too far from the doors
Of a copious and ample choice
Of 24-hour stores.

I must go down to the shops again,
For the call of the spending spree
Is a wild call and a clear call
That strongly appeals to me;
And all I ask is a clear aisle
And a trolley whose wheels run true,
And goods piled high for me to buy,
And a checkout without a queue.

I must go down to the shops again
For some retail therapy.
I must shop 'til I drop for if I should stop
What would become of me?
And all I ask is my card should work
When it comes time to pay,
For like Scarlet O'Hara I firmly believe
Tomorrow's another day.

*

47

The Courier

'Is there anybody there?' said the courier,
Knocking on the glazed front door;
And his van on the tarmac spewed out gases
From somewhere beneath its floor:
Condensation blew out of a boiler,
Above the courier's head:
And he smote upon the door again a second time;
'Is there anybody there?' he said.
But no one descended to the courier;
No head from PVC sill
Leaned over and looked into his grey eyes,
Where he stood perplexed and still.
But only a disabled old lady
That dwelt in the lone house then
Was descending in the quiet of the staircase
To that voice from the world of men:
On the slow moving stairlift sat waiting
To get down to the empty hall,
Hearkening in an air stirred and shaken
By the impatient courier's call.
Then he suddenly smote on the door, even
Louder, and lifted his head:-
'Tell them I came, and no one answered,
And that I left a card,' he said.
He hastily scribbled a postcard:
'Sorry you were out,' it read,
'I have left your package in the safe place,
Behind the wheelie bin by the shed.'
Ay, she heard his foot upon the pathway,
And the sound of an engine cough,
And how the silence surged softly backward,
When the Transit van drove off.

*

48

The Walrus and the Carpenter

The Walrus and the Carpenter
Were walking down the Strand.
Said the Walrus to the Carpenter,
"Am I to understand
That at the next election
You still intend to stand?"

"I must do," said the Carpenter,
"Bring members to their senses,
They're beset with their divisions
And need to mend their fences.
I'll do it without a thought of gain,
Though of course there are expenses."

"What if you," the Walrus asked,
"Should lose if you compete?
You'd have no leg to stand on
If they're voting with their feet;
But notwithstanding that, you have
To stand to get a seat.

"Are you sure," the Walrus asked,
"You want to join that lot?
They don't inspire confidence,
And spout a lot of rot."
The Carpenter thought for a bit,
And answered, "Well, why not?

"I fancy I could have a bright
Political career.
Once I am elected then
My thoughts I could make clear."
The Walrus shook his head and said,
"That's not a good idea.

"An MP must not ever say
Exactly what he means.
Circumlocution has to be
Embedded in his genes."
"In that case," said the Carpenter,
"I'm blown to smithereens."

"I wonder if," the Walrus asked,
"Your principles you'd keep?
When dining with good Doctor Faust
The price can be quite steep."
"They'll hang me," sighed the Carpenter,
"For lamb, so why not sheep?

"And if in time my leader is
Impressed with my success,
I might get a promotion as
Reward for my prowess;
Or as a second afterthought,
Be made a PPS."

"They baffle me," the Walrus said.
"What's going through their dome?
As soon as they are in the House,
They buy a second home.
If asked how this is justified,
They murmur, 'When in Rome.'

"To fall out with their leader they
Go through a diff'rent door,
They sit on diff'rent benches, or
They even cross the floor.
Such empty gestures are not what
They were elected for.

"They nearly all make speeches, but
The Speaker is the one
Who just sits there in silent thought.
Of action there is none;
Not one of them does anything,
When all is said and done.

"Their grasp of mathematics
One cannot but deride:
To find the larger of two sums
They frequently divide."
"Such folly," said the Carpenter,
"I simply won't abide."

"The best advice that I can give –
Your principles must come first;
But pragmatism often means
Priorities get reversed.
So left or right, remain or stay,
You'll be forever cursed."

The Carpenter had listened
To all the Walrus said,
And his dire admonitions
Were now swimming in his head.
"If that's an MP's life," he thought,
"I would preferably be dead."

So, "Thank you," said the Carpenter,
"I think I've changed my mind.
I'll treat you to some oysters
Since you have been so kind.
So let's away along the Strand
And leave politics behind."

*

49

Hinda's Gazelle

She never nursed a dear gazelle
But it was sure to die.
Was there no-one there to tell
Hinda the reason why?

She sighed into its helpless face -
It met an early death.
An obvious, though tragic, case
Of virulent bad breath.

She had no better luck with flowers.
Chrysanthemums and roses
Fell prey within a few short hours
To Hinda's halitosis.

I blame her friends – far too polite.
They should have been much bolder.
With nose averted to the right,
Her best friend should have told her!

*

50

Fatherly Advice

Polonius to Laertes:

What, you still here? But yet before you go
I'll bend your ear with fatherly advice.
Since the apparel oft proclaims the man,
Do not wear trainers with a three-piece suit
Nor tuck your vest into your underpants.
Neither a follower nor a leader be,
But keep a low profile in middle rank.
When those in charge cry "Forward!" mind you go
Most hastily to safety in the rear.
And whatever else you do, my son,
Don't ever, ever, ever volunteer.
This above all: to thine own self be true,
And it must follow, as the night the day,
Thou canst then lie barefaced to any man.
Be thou well lettered, not illiterate.
Take care you always mind your p's and q's
And cross your t's and dot your i's. OK?
I turn now to temptations of the flesh.
Those jeunes filles and those midinettes
Are out to trap you. Take the sage advice
Of wise Ben Franklin, who has well described
The benefits of courting older dames.
Don't stay too long in France, come back and fight
For young Ophelia's honour, which is more
Than she herself has done, from what I hear.
I've no idea what she intends - to live
In Elsinore or else in sin to live?
And if on blasted moor three crones you meet
Who promise a Great Dane someday you'll be,
You'd be barking mad if you don't see
That that's a different play entirely.

Laertes to Polonius:

> Thanks, Pop, for the advice. I'll bear in mind
> What you have said. Now here is mine to you
> Before I take the Eurostar to Paris:
> Take care, mind how you go, and watch your arras!

*

51

R v Sir John Doe

Magistrate: What's the first case?

Clerk of the Court: R v Sir John Doe, your honour. Vagrancy and harassment.

Magistrate: Sir John Doe? Is that really his name?

Clerk of the Court: No, sir. He refused to give his name, so we put him in as John Doe, but then he claimed to be a knight at arms, so we made it Sir John Doe to be on the safe side.

Magistrate: Oh, all right. Well, let's hear the prosecution then.

Prosecuting Solicitor: Defendant is charged with loitering, your honour.

Magistrate: Loitering? With intent?

Prosecuting Solicitor: No, your honour, it is not alleged that he had any criminal intent, just that he was loitering.

Magistrate: In what way was he loitering, then?

Prosecuting Solicitor: Palely, your honour.

Magistrate: Palely, eh? Any accomplices?

Prosecuting Solicitor: No, your honour, he was alone.

Magistrate *[writing a note]*: "Alone, and palely loitering." Proceed.

Prosecuting Solicitor: It is also alleged that he has been making a nuisance of himself with a young lady, your honour.

Magistrate: Very well, let's hear what the defendant has to say for himself. *[Turns to defendant in the dock.]* Now then, you've heard what has been alleged. Why do you behave like that? What is the matter with you? What can ail thee?

Defendant *[haggard and woe-begone]*: It all began when I met this woman.

Magistrate: Ah, the old femme fatale, eh? Where did you meet her?

Defendant: In the meads it was. I gave her everything, garlands, bracelets, scent. I even let her ride my horse.

Magistrate: And did she welcome your attentions?

Defendant: At first she did. She used to sing to me, and do this thing with her body.

Magistrate: What thing?

Defendant: Well, sort of bending sideways in a seductive manner. And when we made love, she made appreciative noises, moaning like, sweetly.

Magistrate: And what happened to change all that?

Defendant: Well, without any warning, she slipped me a mickey.

Magistrate: What is a mickey?

Prosecuting Solicitor: Mickey is a colloquial expression, your honour, for a drink laced with a psychoactive drug or incapacitating agent, usually chloral hydrate.

Magistrate: Thank you. *[To the defendant]* What made you think that she had drugged you?

Defendant: She took me to her place . . .

Magistrate: Where was that?

Defendant: The elfin grot, it was. And there she fed me strange plants and stuff to eat, and it gave me the weirdest visions, and I passed out.

Magistrate: Hmm, sounds to me more like magic mushrooms than a mickey. What sort of visions?

Defendant: Pale kings, pale princes, pale warriors, all deathly pale.

Magistrate *[to the Clerk of the Court]*: Is the lady in court?

Clerk of the Court: Yes, your honour.

Magistrate: Have her take the stand.

[Belle, an opulently built lady, saunters across the court with swinging hips and enters the witness box.]

Magistrate: State your name.

Belle: Just my name? I'm usually asked for my telephone number too.

Magistrate: Just your name.

Belle: Okay, judge. It's Belle.

Magistrate: And your surname?

Belle: No surname, judge, just Belle, though I have been called Belle of the Nineties, and sometimes Ding Dong Belle.

Magistrate: Ding Dong Belle? Why are you called that?

Belle: For a couple of reasons, judge. *[She leans forward over the rail of the witness box and gently shakes her shoulders.]*

Magistrate: Harrumph! Now then, are you acquainted with the accused?

Belle: Sure am.

Magistrate: And what are your feelings towards him?

Belle: Well, at first I really took a shine to him. As soon as I met him I knew I could make him my lover. I'm like that; I take a man as I find him; and if I find him, I take him. But then I was told that he was two-timing me, having it off with that Lady Guinevere – well, she calls herself a lady, but from what I've heard . . .

Magistrate: Never mind that. So what did you do?

Belle: Well, I didn't think he deserved any mercy, so I gave him the brush-off, natch. But he wouldn't take no for an answer. I gave him a little something to cool his ardour, but he still kept loitering palely around the place, so I turned him in.

Magistrate: Thank you. You may step down, but before you go, Miss Belle, leave your telephone number with the Clerk of the Court, just for the record, you understand, a mere formality.

Belle: Sure, I understand, judge. *[Winks at him.]* Say, you're OK, you can come up and see me anytime.

[She leaves the box. The magistrate addresses the accused.]

Magistrate: I find you guilty on both counts, but as there seem to be some extenuating circumstances, on the first count I am giving you a conditional discharge. The conditions are these: First, you must let the Salvation Army or Social Services find you somewhere to live. Good Heavens, man, it's late October already. The harvest is in, the song birds have all flown south, the sedge on the lake has all withered, the squirrels are stocked up ready to hibernate. It should be obvious to you what that means: it's nearly winter. Get a roof over your head while you can.

The second condition is that you find yourself something to do, instead of all this moping around. You could slay a few dragons, for example, or search for the Holy Grail, or rescue maidens in distress.

The third condition is that you see a doctor and get him to prescribe a course of iron tablets. I strongly suspect that you are anaemic, otherwise your loitering wouldn't be so pale.

On the second count, I am issuing a restraining order banning you from approaching within 200 yards of Miss Belle. So keep away from her! If I catch you anywhere near her – I mean of course, if you breach that order you will be liable to severe penalties. You may go.

[To the Clerk of the Court] Next case, please.

R v Blessed Damozel

Clerk of the Court: The next case is R v Blessed Damozel, your honour, soliciting and indecent exposure.

Magistrate: Let us hear from the prosecuting solicitor then. What is the defendant alleged to have done?

Prosecuting Solicitor: She leaned out, your honour.

Magistrate: Leaned out? Where from?

Prosecuting Solicitor: From the gold bar of the house she was occupying, your honour.

Magistrate: Leaned out from the gold bar? Nothing illegal in that is there?

Prosecuting Solicitor: Not per se, your honour. The gravamen of the case revolves around the condition of the defendant's robe when she leaned out.

Magistrate: And what was that?

Prosecuting Solicitor: It was ungirt, your honour.

Magistrate: Ungirt?

Prosecuting Solicitor: From clasp to hem, your honour.

Magistrate: Ungirt from clasp to hem? What, all the way?

Prosecuting Solicitor: All the way, your honour.

Magistrate: (pensively): Well, well, all the way! And was she . . . ?

Prosecuting Solicitor: Not a stitch, your honour. You can imagine the effect.

Magistrate: I can imagine it. I am imagining it. My word! Clasp to hem, eh? And not a stitch. Phew! Is it getting warm in here? Usher, open some windows please. Clasp to hem! It's no good, it's too hot in here to continue. Case adjourned! This sitting is adjourned! Clear the court! *[sotto voce to the Clerk of the Court]* See if that Belle dame is still in the building, and if she is free for lunch.

*

Apologies and/or homage are due to the following poets, whose works have been re-visited in this book:

William Blake (1757-1827)
Robert Browning (1812-1889)
Robert Burns (1759-1796)
Lord Byron (1788-1824)
Lewis Carroll (1832-1898)
Arthur H. Clough (1819-1861)
Samuel Taylor Coleridge (1772-1834)
Allan Cunningham (1784-1842)
Walter De la Mare (1873-1956)
Marriott Edgar (1880-1951)
Edward FitzGerald (1809-1883)
Felicia Dorothea Hemans (1793-1835)
W.E. Henley (1849-1903)
Robert Herrick (1591-1674)
A. E. Houseman (1859-1936)
Leigh Hunt (1784-1859)
John Keats (1795-1821)
Alan J. Lerner (1918-1986)
Henry Wadsworth Longfellow (1807-1882)
Christopher Marlowe (1564-1593)
John Masefield (1878-1967)
Thomas Moore (1779-1852)
Christina Rossetti (1830-1894)
Dante Gabriel Rossetti (1828-1882)
William Shakespeare (1564-1616)
Sir John Suckling (1609-1641)
Alfred, Lord Tennyson (1809-1892)
Dylan Thomas (1914-1953)
Walt Whitman (1819-1892)
Charles Wolfe (1791-1823)
William Wordsworth (1770-1850)

*

Index of first lines of original poems

Poem No.

28	When we two parted	(Lord Byron)
29	Once did she hold the gorgeous East in fee	(Wm. Wordsworth)
30	Awake! For morning in the bowl of night	(Edward Fitzgerald)
31	Three years she grew in sun and shower	(William Wordsworth)
32	I wandered lonely as a cloud	(William Wordsworth)
33	Break, break, break	(Alfred, Lord Tennyson)
34	The Grand Old Duke of York	(Traditional)
35	N/A	
36	In Xanadu did Kubla Khan	(Samuel Taylor Coleridge)
37	O Captain! my Captain! our fearful trip is done	(Walt Whitman)
38	Do not go gentle into that good night	(Dylan Thomas)
39	I wish I loved the human race	(Sir Walter Raleigh)
40	When icicles hang by the wall	(William Shakespeare)
41	Much have I travelled in the realms of gold	(John Keats)
42	Does the road wind uphill all the way	(Christina Rossetti)
43	N/A	
44	O my love is like a red, red rose	(Robert Burns)
45	Myself when young did eagerly frequent	(Edward Fitzgerald)
46	I must go down to the seas again	(John Masefield)
47	"Is there anyone there?" said the Traveller	(Walter de la Mare)
48	The sun was shining on the sea	(Lewis Carroll)
49	From 'The Fire Worshippers'	(Thomas Moore)
50	Hamlet. Act 1, scene 3.	(William Shakespeare)
51	O what can ail thee, knight at arms	(John Keats)
	The Blessed Damozel lean'd out	(Dante G. Rossetti)

*

About the Authors

Ken Kelsey is a retired Chartered Secretary and Barrister, and one of the dwindling number of Bletchley Park Veterans. His published works include The Ultimate Book of Number Puzzles, published by Random House; and The Nutcombe Papers; Sophie's Odyssey; A Beginner's Guide to Magic Squares and Cubes; and A Book of Humorous Poems, all available through Amazon.

David Kelsey graduated in law from The Queen's College, Oxford, and served in H.M. Overseas Civil Service in the Gold Coast. He returned to the UK and was employed in local government for thirty years. In retirement his interests have included film noir and research into the Crimean War, some results of which can be seen at www.kelsey.me.uk.

*

49442464R00050

Made in the USA
Columbia, SC
22 January 2019